Mount Rushmore
National Memorial

W0009097

Unknown

Alpha Editions

This edition published in 2023

ISBN : 9789357950237

Design and Setting By
Alpha Editions
www.alphaedis.com
Email - info@alphaedis.com

Contents

Contents

FOREWORD

A monument's dimensions should be determined by the importance to civilization of the events commemorated. We are not here trying to carve an epic, portray a moonlight scene, or write a sonnet; neither are we dealing with mystery or tragedy, but rather the constructive and the dramatic moments or crises in our amazing history. We are cool-headedly, clear-mindedly setting down a few crucial, epochal facts regarding the accomplishments of the Old World radicals who shook the shackles of oppression from their light feet and fled despotism to people a continent: who built an empire and rewrote the philosophy of freedom and compelled the world to accept its wiser, happier forms of government.

We believe the dimensions of national heartbeats are greater than village impulses, greater than city demands, greater than state dreams or ambitions. Therefore, we believe a nation's memorial should, like Washington, Jefferson, Lincoln and Roosevelt, have a serenity, a nobility, a power that reflects the gods who inspired them and suggests the gods they have become.

As for sculptured mountains—

Civilization, even its fine arts, is, most of it, quantity-produced stuff; education, law, government, wealth—each is enduring only as the day. Too little of it lasts into tomorrow and tomorrow is strangely the enemy of today, as today has already begun to forget buried yesterday. Each succeeding civilization forgets its predecessor, and out of its body builds its homes, its temples. Civilizations are ghouls. Egypt was pulled apart by its successor; Greece was divided among the Romans; Rome was pulled to pieces by bigotry and a bitterness much of which was engendered in its own empire building.

I want, somewhere in America on or near the Rockies, the backbone of the Continent, so far removed from succeeding, selfish, coveting civilizations, a few feet of stone that bears witness, carries the likenesses, the dates, a word or two of the great things we accomplished as a Nation, placed so high it won't pay to pull down for lesser purposes.

Hence, let us place there, carved high, as close to heaven as we can, the words of our leaders, their faces, to show posterity what manner of men they were. Then breathe a prayer that these records will endure until the wind and the rain alone shall wear them away.

Gutzon Borglum

THE MIGHTY WORKS OF BORGLUM
By RUPERT HUGHES

How big is great? How high is up?

In the wide and numberless fields of creative art, size is a matter of spirit rather than of material bulk. A sonnet may be a masterpiece, and an epic rubbish; or an epic may be sublime, a sonnet petty.

It is only affectation to confine one's praise to small things. Because a poet delights in a brook chuckling through a thicket of birches he need not therefore despise Niagara. The word "colossal" should not be surrendered entirely to the advertisers.

The Shakespeare of the sonnets wrote also "Hamlet" and "King Lear." The Beethoven who wrote the giggling *Scherzos* wrote also the titanic Ninth and added its mighty chorus. Michelangelo did statuettes and sonnets, but also his "Day of Judgment" and his prodigious horned Moses.

To the sincere artist it is the idea that is vital. Once that has inflamed him, he seeks only to give it the shape and the size that its nature dictates.

So Gutzon Borglum, being sensitive to all the moods of life, a born poet, with an innate love of form for its own sake, quick to glow with inspirations of every kind and determined to give each its unique and eloquent shape, has painted and carved without fear or favor the exquisite and the tremendous with equal fidelity.

His genius shines in the little bas-relief of a nymph; in sardonic gargoyles; in the tiny yet epic statuette of the dying Nero, a bloated coward tangled in his toga and drooping to his ignoble death; in the suave portrait of the seated Ruskin; the pathos of the old Boer warrior; in the billowy rush of the stampeding "Mares of Diomedes"; in his colossal head of Lincoln; in his war memorial for Newark, New Jersey, with its marvellously composed forty-two figures and two horses; his magnificent plan for the Stone Mountain, whose thwarting is one of the great tragedies of art; and finally in his supreme achievement, the Mount Rushmore Memorial, where he brought his art to the mountains and left there the four great faces for all eternity.

This unparalleled accomplishment seems to have been not so much the carving of those vast heads upon the peaks as the beating away of the veiling, smothering stone and the releasing of the imprisoned statesmen so that they might look out upon the world and utter their lofty messages in a silence more pervasive and sonorous than any trumpet-tone.

The heads stand up there against the clouds like cloud-gods. Yet they are not offered as gods, but as plain men who glorified the plain man. Each of them is greater in magnitude than the so-called Egyptian Sphinx. The Sphinx represented an unanswerable riddle and she cruelly destroyed all who could not answer it. But these presidents of ours represent brave, clear thinking towards safety and dignity and happiness for all mankind.

The Sphinx was really a portrait, the largest portrait ever made till Borglum came along. It is the head of King Khafre set on the body of a crouching lion guarding the king's tomb, with his pyramid back of it. Khafre had it built during a reign that ended over four thousand, seven hundred and fifty years ago.

Near the Sphinx and Khafre's pyramid is the greater pyramid of King Khufu, better known to us as Cheops. He lived from 2898 to 2875 BC. and his pyramid contains over two million blocks of stone, of an average weight of two and a half tons. Herodotus was told that it took a hundred thousand men twenty years to build it.

Near Karnak there are still standing—or sitting—two portrait statues of Amenhotep III, who ruled fourteen hundred years B.C.—just about the time of Moses. These statues are seventy feet high.

One of the four colossal statues at Abu Simbel represents Rameses II, who died about two thousand, six hundred years ago. Lying on its side is a broken statue of Rameses II, once 90 feet high and carved from a single thousand-ton block. This and another statue of him in granite ninety feet high were, according to Breasted writing in 1905, "the greatest monolithic statues ever executed."

But Borglum's bust of Washington is larger than the whole figure of Rameses, Lincoln's nose is 21 feet long and the sparkle in his eye is secured by a block of granite thirty inches long.

Some of the Egyptian portraits were carved upon their cliffs somewhat as Borglum's statues are upon the peaks. At Abu Simbel there are four such statues of enormous bulk.

The Assyrians also built huge monuments, and inscribed the texts of whole histories on the faces of cliffs. Their kings were usually represented as enormous winged bulls with the heads of bearded men. These were called, strangely enough, "cherubs."

The Greeks created for their greater gods statues of gold and ivory—whence the epithet "chryselephantine." Such was the colossal Zeus that Pheidias made for Olympia. It was about fifty feet high. Pheidias made also two colossal figures of Athena for Athens, one in bronze that stood up like a lighthouse and was visible to sailors far out to sea. The other had ivory flesh and robes of gold, and was seventy feet high.

The famous bronze Colossus of Rhodes, erected about 274 B.C. by Chares of Lindus, was 105 feet high. It did not straddle a stream, as tradition has it. Half a century after it was set up, an earthquake overthrew it; in 656 A.D. it was sold for junk and carried off by a caravan of 900 camels.

In China one still sees enormous Buddhas, and in our own world the Mayan monstrosities are being brought back from the jungle that swallowed them like a sea.

The statue of Liberty—a gift to us from France—is 151 feet high; with its pedestal it is 305 feet tall.

But none of the giants ancient or modern has approached the size of the greater works of Borglum.

This carver of mountains was himself a mountainy man, born in the mountainous state of Idaho on March 25, 1871. His full name was John Gutzon de la Mothe Borglum. His parents had come over from Denmark. His father, at first a woodcarver, became a physician and surgeon, also a breeder of horses on a 6000-acre ranch. He had no money to give his children, but he gave them a love of form and a knowledge of the horse that not only inspired Gutzon Borglum to some of his most magnificent work, but also made a splendid career for his younger brother, Solon. Solon took fire from Gutzon's fire, worked his way to Paris, won honors there, and came home to his West where he turned out a stream of important sculptures that perpetuate many poignant phases of Western life. His life was suddenly ended in 1922 by an attack of acute appendicitis.

Gutzon's indomitable will carried him from the Idaho ranch to an art school in San Francisco, thence to Paris. He began as both painter and sculptor and was accepted as both by the French salons. In England, critics and royalty heaped honors on him. After painting a series of murals for a big hotel at Leeds and another series for a concert hall at Manchester, he began to abandon the brushes for the chisel, and to turn out statuary in almost every field and almost every imaginable form.

From the first, his works won the highest honors. The Metropolitan Museum bought his "Mares of Diomedes" at once and the French Government promptly purchased a partial replica of it for the Luxembourg Gallery. Commissions rained on him and there was never any repetition in the spirit or treatment of his responses.

There is not space here for even a catalogue of his triumphs. He also wrote much and well. He was an engineer and an inventor, overcoming by his own skill supposedly unconquerable problems involved in the construction of his larger works. He was an orator of eloquence with a practical skill in politics. At times he was a statesman and the close associate of Paderewski and Masaryk in their re-creation of their lost republics. During the first World War he investigated and exposed the causes for a mysterious and dangerous failure in American aircraft manufacture. His career has a strange kinship in its versatility with that of Leonardo da Vinci, and I believe that his name will live as long.

In 1909 he married Mary Montgomery, a distinguished scholar in ancient Oriental languages, and a translator of cuneiform inscriptions. A son and a daughter blessed this union of two great souls.

It was in 1907 that I first met Gutzon Borglum while preparing an article on his work, to which I paid complete homage. This was the beginning of a lifelong friendship of which I wrote him while he was glorifying the South Dakota mountains:

"I have always had an awe and a reverence for you that fought with my love for the simple, jovial, twinkling-eyed friend you always were."

He answered: "You have said your say about me and it is a wet eye that reads through the letter. You know how vandalism in the name of Civilization raids the tombs of our ancestors and destroys the records of History. One of my motives in this work was to carve these records of our great West-World adventure as high into the heavens as I could find the stone."

As man and as sculptor he was passionately American and he has not only given to his country monuments of art that equal the greatest of other nations, but he has given artistic expression to the ideals that make America America.

The Sphinx and its temple have only recently been recovered from the sand that submerged them for thousands of years. Yet even now the worst tyrannies and cruelties of the Pharaohs have been revived and paralleled in Europe, just as our gentlest, noblest ideals were to be found co-existing with savagery in ancient Egypt.

I hope, I believe that in 7000 A.D. there will be pilgrimages to Mount Rushmore by Americans still keeping alive the flames of freedom kindled and rekindled by the four heroes Borglum had immortalized, immortalizing himself and his and their ideals along with them.

His Mount Rushmore Memorial presents to posterity four great Americans who upheld the rights and equalities of all mankind, and who were themselves the very personifications of Americanism.

Their noble heads are lofty enough to mingle with the clouds, and the parading lights of sun and moon and stars, and the processionals of rain and snow and mist give them a beauty that is always changing yet everlastingly changeless.

Only a great soul and a great artist could have conceived or achieved such a monument to them and to himself. His gifts of spirit and execution were, I feel, unsurpassed by anything of their kind in the history of the world.

The Memorial in winter with a light fall of snow softening the surrounding landscape.

FROM THE BEGINNING
By MRS. GUTZON BORGLUM

A nation's memorials are a record of its civilization and the artist who builds them is the instrument of his time. He is inspired by the same forces that influence the nation's destiny—the greater the period, the greater the art. The artist cannot escape his destiny. Like the "Hound of Heaven" it "pursues him down the years," forces him to leave his home, to go into exile, to combat mountains even, to accomplish what must be.

How else can we explain why a man should abandon a comfortable way of life, among pleasant surroundings, to hurl himself against a gigantic rock, to cling like a human fly to a perpendicular peak, to struggle with hostile human nature, in order to carve against the sky a record of the great experiment in democracy on this continent—a record which will live on and be an inspiration to future generations, a shrine to be visited, even after the thing it commemorated may have passed.

This is the history of Rushmore told in a few words. The contributing factors are of interest and should be related but two outstanding facts are that a few kindred souls, giants in their day, fostered a form of democratic government and established a great nation and that a hundred and fifty years later another group of Americans realized the importance of making a record in the granite for all time of what manner of men they were and what they achieved.

The initial step in this great enterprise was taken by Doane Robinson, state historian of South Dakota, who had heard of the monument being carved in Georgia by Gutzon Borglum to honor the heroes of the South in the war between the states and thought it would be a fine idea to have a similar patriotic shrine in South Dakota to bring that state to the attention of the nation.

Mr. Robinson invited Mr. Borglum in 1924 to visit the Black Hills to see what could be done. The first thought was to carve the likeness of Washington and perhaps of Lincoln in one of the granite upthrusts known as the Needles. The stone, however, was not suitable and there was no special reason for memorializing Washington and Lincoln as individual presidents in South Dakota. Then Mr. Robinson told the sculptor of a lead tablet discovered by children playing near old Fort Pierre, which had been planted there in 1743 by Verendrye, an emissary of Louis of

France, sent to establish French territory behind the English. This fired his imagination. Here was a subject for the great memorial he wanted to carve in the Hills.

South Dakota lies in the heart of the old Louisiana Territory, purchased by Jefferson in 1803, in order to control the mouth of the Mississippi, which marked the first step away from the Atlantic seaboard colonies in the expansion of the little republic. That step led to the establishment of Texas, the conquest of California, the acquisition of Oregon and Alaska and the spanning of the continent from ocean to ocean by the empire nation called the United States. This was a subject worthy of a mountain—a monument to a nation, to its philosophy of government, its ideals and aspirations, its great leaders. Here in this remote spot, protected by its inaccessibility from the vandalism of succeeding generations, would be carved a Shrine of Democracy, as an imperishable record of a great people.

Here is Mt. Rushmore as it stood for countless ages before the poetic and patriotic idea of the great national memorial was born in the mind of Gutzon Borglum.

Mr. Borglum paid a second and third visit to the Hills and camped among them for two weeks, exploring and examining every rock large enough to suggest a monument, with the result that the huge granite upthrust called Mount Rushmore was selected as the only stone sound enough to be suitable for carving. Another reason for choosing Rushmore was the important consideration of lighting. It was imperative that the cliff on which the figures were to be carved should face the east in order to get the maximum amount of sunlight all the day long. Washington's face is so placed that it catches the first rays of light in the morning and reflects the last ruddy glow in the evening. Many beautiful works of art are made insignificant by poor lighting.

Senator Peter Norbeck, who had created the park system of South Dakota and played an important part in the creation of the Rushmore Memorial, also agreed that, in spite of its remote position with only riding trails leading to it, there was no other location possible.

Ranging downward like spiders swinging on fine threads, workmen made the strokes on the granite mountainside which now bears the features of George Washington.

Scaffolding suspended from cables enabled the workmen to reach down from the brow of the mountain in order to carry on their courageous and difficult labors.

That autumn a group of Rapid City women put on a pageant of flags, designed by Mr. Borglum, on the top of the cliff to show the different epochs through which the territory had passed. The French flag was first hoisted, then the Spanish, then the flag of Napoleon, next the colonial flag and finally the present flag of the United States. Thus was Mount Rushmore officially dedicated to the Memorial. Mr Borglum then returned to his temporary studio in San Antonio, Texas, to make the models and decide what characters best illustrated the idea to which he was trying to give form.

George Washington's presence in the group was inevitable. He was the rock on which the republic was founded—the plumb line to establish its direction. So on Mount Rushmore his head is exactly perpendicular, facing the east, unaffected by the others in the group, the measuring rod determining the position of the others. Equally important with Washington was Thomas Jefferson, the author of the Declaration of Independence. By the purchase of the Louisiana Territory, as stated above, he had taken the first step westward in the course of the nation's growth. He is represented on the mountain as a young man. He was only 33 when he wrote the Declaration of Independence.

Abraham Lincoln, the saviour of the republic, was inevitable in any record of the country's history and finally Theodore Roosevelt was selected because, by cutting the Panama Canal, he had accomplished the dream of Columbus and opened a Sea-way from Europe to Asia and his name was closely linked with the territorial expansion following the war with Spain. He was also the first president to attempt the curbing of big business interests and the only president who had been familiar with the west. He had close associations with South Dakota.

Models in the studio at the foot of the mountain which guided construction of the actual figures (seen through window).

The Mount Harney Memorial Association was authorized in 1925 by the state legislature to undertake the project on Mount Rushmore. No funds were voted for the purpose. Contributions were obtained from the three railroads serving the state, from the Homestake Mine and from private individuals, among them Mr. Charles Rushmore, a New York lawyer, after whom, quite accidentally, the cliff had been named. The work went on slowly, with considerable opposition, until President Coolidge's visit to the Black Hills in 1927. He made a splendid speech at a picturesque ceremony held at Rushmore, immediately following which he took Mr. Borglum aside, inquired about the financing and urged him to come to Washington for help. It is doubtful whether, without this impetus given by President Coolidge, the carving would ever have been accomplished.

The Mount Rushmore National Memorial Commission came into existence as the result of a Congressional Bill, passed on Washington's Birthday in 1929. The act carried an appropriation of $250,000 for the memorial, which was to be matched on a fifty-fifty basis by private subscriptions; it designated Gutzon Borglum as the sculptor and designer of the four figures and provided also for an inscription on the mountain.

The first ascent of the mountain was made up the canyon where the present wooden stairway now is. After the initial survey was made, pine trees with branches cut off and cleats nailed at right angles to the trees were laid in the crevices to serve as ladders. Heavy ropes were then carried by hand to the top and a small winch was carried as far as possible by pack horse and then carried to the top by hand. After this winch was fastened on the top of the mountain, it in turn was used to pull up the heavy cable that became the tramway from the ground to the mountain top. Building material was pulled up and shelters built for the men. A small studio was also built to house the plaster reproductions of the master models that were in the studio at the foot of the mountain. These reproductions were used for measurements to save time required to go to the studio 1500 feet away and 500 feet below. In some cases these models were hung over the side of the mountain so that they could be consulted and compared with the measurements as the actual stone work progressed. By this method it was possible to save considerable time and labor.

Roughing out the face of Theodore Roosevelt. The strong chin and the mouth are already visible. The mass of stone at the top will be carved away to form the mustache.

The work of fitting the figures into the cracked granite upthrust called Mt. Rushmore has been a constant struggle between composition and finding solid stone for each of the four heads.

Close-up of Lincoln. Note the shafts of granite in the eyes of Lincoln. The light reflected by these shafts gives the eyes their lifelike glint when seen from a distance.

In the first design Jefferson was placed at the right of Washington and Lincoln on his left, and Theodore Roosevelt occupied the position now occupied by Lincoln. However serious flaws developed in the stone on this side of Washington; and it therefore became necessary to change our design and place Jefferson to Washington's left. This made it necessary to place Theodore Roosevelt between Jefferson and Lincoln, and the stone had to be removed to a depth of approximately 120 feet from the original surface to get back far enough for the Roosevelt face. The heads were finally relegated to their approximate position (being moved several times as new conditions of the stone developed), that is they were tilted or dropped or made to look more to the right or left as the case might have been, to meet the composition or avoid flaws in the stone. This movement being made simply by moving the respective heads on the model and cutting the stone accordingly. It was not possible to fit the heads so that they would be entirely free from fissures, but it was possible to place them so that none of these fissures would be unsupported from below and that removes the danger of some vital part dropping off. As each head was started its center was located, and at this center point on the top of the head a plate was located. This was graduated in degrees 0 to 360 degrees, and at its center a horizontal arm was located that traversed this horizontal are. This arm was about 30 feet long, in effect a giant protractor laid on top of the head. The arm was graduated in feet and inches so that at any point we could drop a plumb bob from this arm, and by measuring the vertical distance on this plumb line determine exactly the amount of stone to be removed. After determining this master center point on the mountain, we set a smaller arc and arm on our model in the same relative position. With this small device we would make all our measurements on our model and then enlarge them twelve times and transfer them to the large measuring device on the mountain. Thru this system every face had a measurement made every six inches both vertically and horizontally. These measurements were then painted on the stone and it was thru this means that men totally unfamiliar with sculptural form were able to do this undertaking. In fact all the men employed on the work were local men trained by the sculptor.

Pneumatic drills are used for drilling and the compressed air is provided by large compressors located on the ground and driven by electricity. The air is forced or conveyed to the top of the mountain by a 3" pipe and then by the use of smaller pipes and rubber hoses is conveyed to the drills.

Over 400,000 tons of granite have been removed from the mountain in carving the figures, at a total expense of slightly more than $900,000. This includes all building, stairways and machinery.

Workmen putting the finishing touches on the strong face of the Rough-rider President.

The men are let down over the face of the stone in leather swings similar to bos'n chairs used on ships. These swings are fastened on to ⅜" steel cables which are in turn fastened on to winches located on the top of the heads. These winches are operated by hand. There are about seven winches on the top of each head. The men are lowered to their place of work by these winches, taking with them their jackhammers or pneumatic tools and other necessary equipment. One man is located in a position where he can see all the men at work, and is "The Callboy," and has a microphone with a loud speaker at each of the winches and when any of the men working in the swings wants to be raised or lowered they signal this call-boy and he relays the message thru the loud speakers to the winchman. He also keeps the workmen supplied with new drills as they need them, by relaying their requests to the steelman who carries the steel to the men in the swings as it is needed. This steel is used over and over again; as it is dulled it is taken to the blacksmith shop on the ground via the cable car, heated, sharpened, re-heated and tempered and sent back to the mountain again. About 400 of these drills are dulled each day. They drill on an average about four feet before being sharpened. In some places the stone is so hard they will only last or drill about six inches and in other places they will last seven or eight feet before being re-sharpened.

The work in process as it appeared from an odd angle ... from the road running along the side of the mountain. Not many have seen the Memorial from this point of view.

The problem of finance has always been acute in connection with the work of the Rushmore Memorial. The economic hardships of the country made it increasingly difficult to match the Federal appropriation, without which the carving could not go on. The sculptor made repeated trips through the state and beyond its borders to arouse interest in the undertaking. He succeeded in raising some money by publishing a small book about Rushmore. There were never enough funds for as much power or as many men as he would have liked to use. There were long months when the work was stopped altogether. Finally the government took over the whole burden of financing and the work continued regularly, after 1938, being halted only by weather conditions. The sculptor was at last able to employ one or two trained stone carvers to do the finer work of finishing.

The Washington head was unveiled in 1930, with Mr. Cullinan, first chairman of the Rushmore Commission presiding. President Franklin D. Roosevelt came for the unveiling of the Jefferson head in 1936. His unfailing interest and support have insured the finishing of the Memorial. At the unveiling of the face of Abraham Lincoln in 1937, a nation wide radio hookup carried the speeches to all parts of the country and again in 1939, when Governor Bushfield of South Dakota conducted ceremonies celebrating the Golden Jubilee of the State of South Dakota at Mount Rushmore, the radio carried the speeches and music all over the United States. The upper part of the face of Theodore Roosevelt was uncovered at that time.

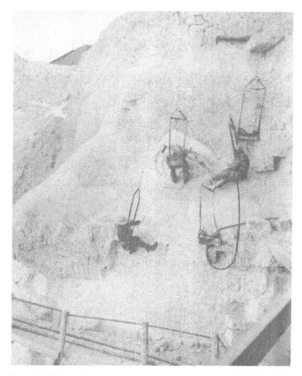

The face of Jefferson begins to take form. The nose and the forehead are already plainly visible, but many tons of stone must be removed before the picture is complete.

Mr. Borglum was always scrupulously careful to protect his men from harm and it was his boast that in all his years of hazardous mountain carving no worker was seriously injured. He took no care of himself, however, and physicians said that undoubtedly the strenuous work of carving at that altitude weakened his heart and in March, 1941, it stopped beating. The carving was practically finished; there remained only the finishing of the hands and hair of the four figures and the Rushmore National Memorial Commission entrusted that work to the sculptor's son, Lincoln Borglum, who had been with his father from the beginning of the work.

A blast is set off. The handling of powder and dynamite was an especially delicate problem, since a single badly placed charge might easily spoil the work of many months.

The faces of the four presidents, as carved on Mount Rushmore, are approximately 60 feet from chin to forehead; if completed from head to foot the figures would be 465 feet high. The entire head of the sphinx in Egypt is not quite as long as Washington's nose. The entire cost of the Memorial, including all expenses of carving, buildings and salaries, is $900,000. This is at the rate of less than two dollars for every ton of stone removed, which is a cost incredibly low considering the hardness of the granite and that every piece must be removed in such a way as not to injure the surface behind. On this investment the Federal Government has received from tourists from the one cent gas tax on the increased sale of gas during the years since the work started over two million dollars and the income to South Dakota is over twenty million dollars annually.

From these beginnings today shine forth the faces of four of the greatest men of American history, to light the path of freedom for countless generations yet to come.

THE ROLE OF THE NATIONAL PARK SERVICE

Millions of Americans and liberty-loving people from all over the world have come to the Black Hills of South Dakota to look upon Gutzon Borglum's *Shrine of Democracy*.

The exact number of visitors to the great granite carvings is not known but each travel season the pilgrimage increases in size.

During the period of construction from 1927 to 1941, when work was under supervision of the Mount Rushmore National Memorial Commission, no accurate records of visitors were kept. Hundreds came each day, however, to keep a fascinated watch over the emergence of the likenesses of the four great presidents from the great stone uplift.

Consecration ceremonies attended by President Coolidge and the unveilings of Washington, Jefferson, Theodore Roosevelt, and Lincoln were attended by thousands of people. Distinguished guests participating in these ceremonies included the late President Franklin D. Roosevelt.

Then in 1939, the Memorial was placed under the supervision of the National Park Service of the Department of Interior. World War II intervened, but in the peace years since the transfer, the flow of visitors has been measured at close to a half million persons each travel season, 419,817 being reported for the 1947 travel year.

Among the nine great memorials in the National Park Service system, Mount Rushmore, by 1947, had risen from seventh to fourth place in attendance. So far as these memorials are concerned, those reporting larger visitations were the Lincoln Memorial, the Jefferson Memorial, and the Washington Monument, all in the District of Columbia.

As with other national parks, monuments, and memorials, Mount Rushmore was designated for inclusion in the National Park system because it had become a most inspiring site of historic significance.

Its present administration is designed to promote and regulate the use of the memorial area to conserve the scenery and the natural and historical objects and to provide for the enjoyment of it in such a manner as to leave it unimpaired for the enjoyment of future generations.

A total of nearly 1,800 acres of the Federal Game Sanctuary in the Harney National Forest now comprises the memorial area. It is under the administration of Superintendent Harry J. Liek with headquarters at Wind Cave National Park. The memorial is directly under Acting Custodian J. Estes Suter.

A brief description follows for Wind Cave National Park and the three national monuments—the Badlands, Jewel Cave, and Devils Tower—that are embraced in the Black Hills and Badlands area of southwestern South Dakota and northeastern Wyoming.

WIND CAVE NATIONAL PARK

Wind Cave is the most widely known of the many limestone caverns found near the margin of the Black Hills. Discovered in 1881, it was created a national park in 1903. The strong currents of wind that blow alternately in and out of the mouth of the cave suggested its name.

Boundaries of the park were extended twice and now embrace a total of 28,000 acres of federally-owned land, supporting a large buffalo herd in its natural habitat and other wildlife, such as elk, antelope, and deer.

Chief feature of the park is the exceptional limestone cavern, noted for its unique boxwork rarely found in other sections of the world. Other crystalline formations in various color shadings line a series of subterranean passages, known to be at least 10 miles in extent.

BADLANDS NATIONAL MONUMENT

In sharp contrast to the verdant Black Hills country, the White River Badlands, a barren, treeless region, lies about 50 miles east of the western foothills.

Here nature has beautified the earth with all shades of buff, cream, pale green, gold, and rose. Fantastically carved erosion forms rise above the valleys, some of them 150 to 300 feet high.

The constantly shifting color and the weird formations make this a region of strong imaginative appeal.

JEWEL CAVE NATIONAL MONUMENT

A unique coating of dogtooth calcite crystals which sparkle like jewels in the light distinguish Jewel Cave from other crystal caverns in the Black Hills and provided its name.

One of the finest stands of virgin ponderosa pine remaining in the Black Hills is found within the monument which was established in 1908. It was originally part of the present Harney National Forest but was transferred to the National Park Service, by Executive Order, in 1934.

DEVILS TOWER NATIONAL MONUMENT

Another unusual natural phenomenon of the Black Hills country is the Devils Tower across the South Dakota state line in Wyoming. This is a great column of igneous rock towering 1,280 feet above the Belle Fourche river, whose course is near the base. Devils Tower has the distinction of being the first national monument created under the Antiquities Act of 1906. It was established by proclamation of September 24 of that year, by President Theodore Roosevelt.

Devils Tower in Wyoming's western border of the Black Hills National Forest.

THE ANTIQUITY OF MOUNT RUSHMORE
By the late JOSEPH P. CONNOLLY
President, South Dakota School of Mines

At the Battle of the Pyramids, Napoleon is reported to have exhorted his men by saying, "Soldiers, from these pyramids forty centuries look down upon you." From the standpoint of human history four thousand years represent great antiquity indeed. But as one gazes upon the rugged slopes of Mount Rushmore, he is face to face with antiquity beside which the age of the Egyptian pyramids seems but a moment.

How old is the granite of Rushmore? We have a yardstick by which we can measure that quite accurately. Not far from the mountain, in a subsidiary mass of granite, there was found a few years ago a small piece of coal-black, lustrous mineral known as pitchblende or uraninite, of which the chief constituent is the heaviest known element, uranium. We know that uranium continually undergoes atomic disintegration, changing at a slow, but uniform and measurable rate into lighter elements. The end product of this change is the metal lead. If we submit the specimen of pitchblende to chemical analysis, determine how much lead it contains, how much uranium is still left, it is a comparatively simple calculation to determine from the known rate of change, the number of years that have elapsed since the pitchblende came into existence. That experiment has been performed and the result is one billion four hundred and sixty-five million (1,465,000,000) years. Bear in mind that this enormous figure represents the time that has elapsed since the molten rock came to rest at some depth under the surface of the earth, and cooled sufficiently to crystallize into granite. It represents the age of the solid granite.

But, although the granite of which the mountain is composed dates back to a period almost inconceivably remote, Mount Rushmore itself is much younger. We know that all of the granite mountains of the southern Black Hills were carved out of the rocks by the process of erosion. Field evidence indicates that fairly early in the Tertiary period, approximately thirty million years ago, erosion had carved out the topography of the Black Hills into much the same stage as we see it today. Perhaps Mount Rushmore was not fully born in that period; its form may not yet have been completely sculptured under the chisel of time, but we know that its age must be measured in millions of years and not in centuries.

Mount Rushmore is a child of weathering and erosion. They brought the mountain into being and gave it form. But those relentless parents will not be content to leave their child as they fashioned it. They will continue their work of disintegration on the surface of the rock and along the cracks, until eventually they will completely destroy the mountain they formed, and long before the mountain will have been destroyed, the magnificent carvings of man will disappear. "How long," we anxiously ask, "will the carvings endure?" Two processes will tend eventually to destroy the memorial, chemical weathering and physical disintegration.

A typical view from the Needles highway with the Cathedral Spires in the background.

Fantastic formations in the Badlands. The variegated coloring is at its best in the early morning or the late evening.

Chemical weathering will take place very slowly, so slowly that if it were the only destructive process we had to consider, we could with some confidence say that the memorial would endure for hundreds of thousands of years. And the progress of chemical weathering will probably be impeded by the sculpturing of the memorial, for on the figures the rock will be smoother, water will drain off more rapidly instead of penetrating, lichens and other vegetation will not have as secure a foothold as on the natural face of the rock, and thus will not contribute to so great an extent their destructive acids to such waters as do penetrate.

Physical disintegration is somewhat more to be feared. This operates in two ways, by exfoliation due to changes in temperature, and by frost action. Differential stresses set up by unequal expansion and contraction, owing to the poor heat conductivity of granite, tend to spall off or *exfoliate* the surface layers of rock.

When water gets into the cracks and pores of the rocks and freezes, it exerts an enormous pressure, a pressure that will spall off flakes and blocks of rock. The artist and his associates, fully aware of this hazard, have guarded against it. All cracks and fissures have been carefully avoided in the sculpturing so far as is possible. Such as have been impossible to avoid are being sealed to prevent the ingress of water, thus inhibiting to a very large extent both frost action and chemical weathering.

We have traced in part the geological history of the Mount Rushmore region, hoping that by learning something of its past we may predict something of its future. We see the hazards to which the memorial is exposed. We must frankly recognize them and guard against them so far as possible, as it would be folly to ignore them. If the science of geology can do no more in a practical way for mankind than to point out dangers and sound warnings, it does a worth while service. "How long will the memorial last?" Geology cannot answer specifically. An eminent geologist has already given as definite an answer as it is possible to give, and I can do no better than to close by quoting from the address given by the late Dr. C. C. O'Harra at the unveiling of the head of Washington.

"How long will Mount Rushmore last? Many millions of years. The number nobody knows. How long will endure this monumental, sculptured figure of the Father of our Country which today we unveil? One hundred years? Yes. One thousand years? Yes. A hundred thousand years? In all likelihood, yes. A half million years? Possibly so, nobody knows. The time at any rate will be long, far longer than we can readily comprehend. And this doubtless will abundantly suffice."

THE HALL OF RECORDS AND GREAT STAIRWAY
By LINCOLN BORGLUM

The Hall of Records and Stairway have been part of the Memorial plan from the beginning and are provided for in the so-called "Rushmore Bill" of 1938. A good start has been made in the carving of the Hall, which already has been excavated to the extent of seventy feet. Great care has to be exercised in the use of dynamite in carving this hall, as in carving the faces on the mountain, not to injure the stone which is to remain. Careless explosions of large amounts of powder might crumble the walls.

The Hall is located about two thirds of the way up to the mountain: the entrance to it is in a small gorge or canyon, cut by the ice aeons ago, to the right of the carved faces as one looks at them from below. The Hall is on the opposite side of the gorge from the heads and is not under them. The following is quoted from Mr. Borglum's plan.

"The façade to the Hall's entrance is the mountain wall 140 feet high; supporting pylons, cut into the mountain, flank the entrance. The entrance door itself is 12 feet wide and 20 feet high; the walls are plain, dressed granite and of a fine color. I want to finish the inner entrance wall in mosaic of blue and gold lapis. The depth to the door entrance from the outer façade is 20 feet. The door, swung on a six inch offset of the wall, will be of bronze and glass. Small, carefully modeled bronze figures of historic importance from Columbus and Raleigh to the present day will ornament the doors or be modeled into the supporting frame. The walls of the entrance will carry in gilded bronze immediately within the entrance ancient Indian symbols; British, French, Spanish and American seals.

"The floor of the Hall will be 100 by 80 by 32 feet to an arched ceiling. At the height of fifteen feet an historic frieze, four feet wide, will encircle the entire room. Recesses will be cut into these walls to be filled with bronze and glass cabinets, which will hold the records stamped on aluminum sheets, rolled separately and placed in tubes. Busts of our leaders in all human activities will occupy the recesses between the cabinets. The original thought of a hall of human records I developed at Stone Mountain in Georgia and my drawings and full plans are extant; that was never completed.

"The records of electricity, beginning with Franklin, which has given us light, heat, music, the radio, the telegraph, the telephone and controls in power the extent of which we can hardly imagine, must be here, together with the records of literature, the records of travel, immigration, religious development and also the record of perhaps the largest contribution that we have made to humanity, which has been free controlled peace, a government of the people, by and for the people. Struggle as we will that great contribution is today the cause for the real unrest of Europe. Despotism, tyranny of every form is fighting us wherever it can, to take away from humanity the power freedom gives it—the power that freedom has given America.

Opening of a gorge reached by the Great Stairway is the massive twenty-foot-high entrance to the Hall of Records.

"The Hall will be reached by a monumental flight of steps varying from 15 to 20 feet in width, which will ascend the mountain in front, a little to one side of the sculpture, rising from a great granite disk or platform in the canyon below, which may be used as a rostrum from which speakers may address the public occupying the amphitheater facing the great group.

This picture shows the workmen busy in the early stages of the work of carving the Hall of Records from the granite.

"These steps of granite and cement will be provided with seats at intervals of every fifty feet; they will have a five inch rise and an eighteen inch tread. The ascension from the foot of the steps to the floor of the great entrance is four hundred feet; the entrance way from the steps' landing to the great Hall is 190 feet; the floor of this Hall, reached by three steps, is two feet above the floor of the entrance way in the canyon; this to provide for proper drainage."

Owing to repeated requests from important organizations of women, the urging of some senators and congressmen and Mr. Borglum's own realization of the part women have played in the development of our country, plans had been under way for some years to include women in the great Shrine of Democracy. There was no room in the rock which contains the heads of the four presidents and the only other place seemed to be the west wall of the granite cliff, or in the hall of records. To quote again from Mr. Borglum, from a letter written in January 1940: "If we decide that the west side of the mountain is suitable, I am for it. We must work out a design that is fitting and in no sense harmful in the matter of lighting or location to subjects determined upon and I am entirely in favor of carving the faces of two or three women. If that is determined upon, these figures will be near what has been known in the Rushmore Law as the Inscription and there will be a special paragraph given to the work and services of women. The original inscription referred to the framing of the Declaration of Independence; that was Jefferson's work and the second was the Constitution. That was Washington's greatest service. The third dealt with the purchase of the Louisiana Territory and the fourth, fifth, and sixth, the progress towards the south and southwest, involving Florida, Texas and California, which included Arizona, a portion of Nevada, Utah and a portion of Idaho. The seventh paragraph brought in the Oregon cession from England and the purchase of Alaska. There was one paragraph for Lincoln and one for the finishing of the Panama Canal, which was achieved by Theodore Roosevelt.

The corridor leading from the doorway into the Hall of Records, showing the marks of the stonecutters' tools.

"So by these suggestions you will see that a splendid paragraph can be developed for the part women have played in the development of the nation." In another part of the letter Mr. Borglum made a place for women in the Hall of records and even suggested that a special hall might be carved for them, as there is ample rock for many rooms.

Calvin Coolidge had been asked to collaborate on the inscription and wrote the first two paragraphs. Mr. Borglum stood strongly for "Justice" in the wording, whereas Mr. Coolidge insisted upon "Justice under the Law." Newspaper accounts exaggerated the discussion, which unfortunately was terminated by Mr. Coolidge's death.

GEORGE WASHINGTON

In carving the head of George Washington, Mr. Borglum studied all the known portraits of him and drew heavily on certain famous likenesses which he preferred because he believed them most faithful to the character of the man. Borglum was confronted by an extraordinary problem. He had undertaken to place his sculpture on a mountain peak over 6000 feet above sea level. His face of Washington, tall as a five-story building, was to be far up in the sky "where the clouds fold about it like a great scarf, where the stars blink about its head, and the moon hides behind a lock of hair." As Borglum himself pointed out, it has been the practice of the sculptors of history, immediately they departed from the normal dimensions of men, to conventionalize and simplify their faces and to generalize the portraiture, and, in so doing, lose those qualities which gave distinction. Such methods had no appeal to Borglum. Vehemently, he brushed aside "the claptrap standards of Good Enough." The faces he placed upon the mountain to gaze down upon hundreds of generations of mankind must be true, great, and noble faces, and that of Washington would be the gauge of all the rest. Borglum spent thirteen years digging into every corner of Washington's life in order that his portrait might say the last word about the man who is called the Father of his Country. He made an extensive study of his character and was deeply impressed by the picture presented by Thomas Jefferson in the following letter to Dr. Walter Jones, dated at Monticello, January 2, 1814:

I think I knew Gen. Washington intimately and thoroly; and were I called on to delineate his character, it should be in terms like these.

His mind was great and powerful, without being of the very first order; his penetration strong, tho not so acute as that of a Newton, Bacon, or Locke; and as far as he saw, no judgment was ever sounder. It was slow in operation, being little aided by invention or imagination, but sure in conclusion. Hence the common remark of his officers, of the advantage he derived from councils of war, where hearing all suggestions, he selected whatever was best; and certainly no general ever planned his battles more judiciously. But if deranged during the course of the action, if any member of his plan was dislocated by sudden circumstances, he was slow in readjustment. The consequence was that he often failed in the field, and rarely against an enemy in station, as at Boston and York.

He was incapable of fear, meeting personal dangers with the calmest unconcern. Perhaps the strongest feature in his character was prudence, never acting until every circumstance, every consideration, was maturely weighed; refraining if he saw a doubt, but when once decided, going thru with his purpose, whatever obstacles opposed.

His integrity was most pure, his justice the most inflexible I have ever known, no motives of interest or consanguinity, of friendship, or hatred, being able to bias his decision. He was, indeed, in every sense of the words a wise, a good, and a great man. His temper was naturally high toned; but reflection and resolution had obtained a firm and habitual ascendancy over it. If ever, however, it broke its bonds, he was most tremendous in his wrath.

In his expenses he was honorable, but exact; liberal in contribution to whatever promised utility; but frowning and unyielding on all visionary projects and all unworthy calls on his charity. His heart was not warm in its affections; but he exactly calculated every man's value, and gave him a solid esteem proportioned to it.

His person, you know, was fine, his stature exactly what one would wish, his deportment easy, erect and noble; the best horseman of his age, and the most graceful figure that could be seen on horseback. Altho in the circle of his friends, where he might be unreserved with safety, he took a free share in conversation, his colloquial talents were not above mediocrity, possessing neither copiousness of ideas nor fluency of words. In public, when called on for a sudden opinion, he was unready, short, and embarrassed.

Yet he wrote readily, rather diffusely, in an easy and correct style. This he had acquired by conversation with the world, for his education was merely reading, writing, and common arithmetic, to which he added surveying at a later day.

His time was employed in action chiefly, reading little, and that only in agriculture and English history. His correspondence became necessarily extensive, and, with journalizing his agricultural proceedings, occupied most of his leisure hours within doors.

On the whole, his character was, in its mass, perfect, in nothing bad, in few points indifferent; and it may truly be said that never did nature and fortune combine more perfectly to make a man great, and to place him in the same constellation with whatever worthies have merited from man an everlasting remembrance. For his was the singular destiny and merit of leading the armies of his country successfully thru an arduous war, for the establishment of its independence; of conducting its councils thru the birth of a government, new in its forms and principles, until it had settled down into a quiet and orderly train; and of scrupulously obeying the laws thru the whole of his career, civil and military, of which the history of the world furnishes no other example....

THOMAS JEFFERSON

Writing just a century ago, and a few years after Jefferson's death, one of his earliest biographers said that it had been that statesman's fate "to be at once loved and praised by his friends, and more hated and reviled by his adversaries than any of his compatriots." The fact that much the same could be said of the writing about him today merely shows that the man is still alive in so far as his influence is both felt and feared. So is his great antagonist Hamilton. These two exponents of contrasted philosophies of government, though dead, yet live and are in the thick of the fight today. The issues for which they fought with all their strength are not yet settled. Indeed these issues have broadened and deepened until one in especial has become perhaps the most burning of all in a bewildered and angry world, the question whether the people can govern themselves or must be governed.

Although a political philosopher, Jefferson never set forth his views in any formal treatise, as did John Adams in his voluminous works or Hamilton in *The Federalist*. Probably the most widely read man of his time in America, Jefferson had a broader range of interests—political, religious, economic, agricultural, aesthetic and scientific—than did any other of the leaders. His curiosity was insatiable, but in spite of what has so frequently been asserted, usually by his enemies, although sometimes by his friends, he was not a mere theorist. He kept his feet on the ground. It was the practical application of ideas and their practical effects which appealed most to him and not the ideas in themselves as viewed by a philosopher. Even when he could not use the touchstone of experiment in such matters as his belief in the common man or religious freedom, he was never a doctrinaire. He not only believed but said over and over that government and institutions had to be suited to a people of any given time and place and could not be true or good everywhere and always.

We do not look to Jefferson for a theory of government or of the state. To a great extent the things he had to say about government, and the things for which he strove in his active political life, were based on the America of his day and the slowly developing agricultural one which he envisaged in the future, writing as he did, before the machine age. What gave Jefferson his profound importance in his own day, as it does now, was his view of human life. He was, and still is, the greatest and most influential American exponent of both Liberalism and Americanism.

Liberalism is rather an attitude than a program. It is less a solution of governmental problems than it is a way of looking at them. It is based on the doctrine of live and let live. The Liberal is willing to take risks feared by both Conservatives and Socialists. Not being a fool, he realizes, as do the others, that society must have a structure; but he is more concerned with the freedom and fullness of the life of the citizen within that structure than with the structure itself.

It may also be noted that even in his native Virginia, Jefferson antagonized many of the most important interests and families by what was considered his undermining of a social order. His struggle to break down entail and primogeniture, to free religion from the fetters of a State church, and his well-known opposition to slavery, have not even yet been forgiven by many Virginians who feel that the downfall of the, in many ways, charming and delightful society of the eighteenth century was due to one whom they consider a renegade from his own order. As we shall see later, when Jefferson was involved in financial difficulties in his old age, the citizens of his own State, unlike many elsewhere, did not offer him the slightest aid.

Europe, in the early days of our country, was filled with restraints and barriers. Jefferson felt that the America of his day offered a unique opportunity in the annals of mankind to try out the great experiment of self-government on an unprecedented scale. His Americanism, written in part into the Declaration of Independence, which he preached throughout life by word and act, grew out of his personal experience of America itself. In so far as those qualities of the American people which we group under the word "Americanism" have been fostered by any one man, in addition to the natural forces of the American environment, Jefferson is beyond question that man.

The struggle going on almost everywhere today, in our own country no less than in some of those others which have already lost their liberties, is the struggle between the conception of a strong centralized state controlling the lives of the citizens for the sake of economics and national power, and the conception of personal liberty affording the greatest possible scope for the individual to live his life as he wills. The old questions which Jefferson and Hamilton fought over were who is to rule, why are they to rule, what is the object of their rule? These are now being fought out again, as they always have been, but with increasing bitterness among vast masses of populations. That is why both men are living today and why it is worth while to consider again the life particularly of the one who laid more stress upon freedom and toleration for the individual than on the strength of national power.

JAMES TRUSLOW ADAMS *from "The Living Jefferson," 1936*

ABRAHAM LINCOLN

Carlyle once said to Holman Hunt: "I'm only a poor man, but I would give one third of what I possess for a veritable, contemporaneous representation of Jesus Christ. Had those carvers of marble chiseled a faithful statue of the Son of Man, as he called himself, and shown us what manner of man he was like, what his height, what his build, and what the features of his sorrow-marked face were, I for one would have thanked the sculptor with all the gratitude of my heart for that portrait as one of the most precious heirlooms of the ages."

Remarkable as it may seem, were it not for photography and one life mask, this, with equal truth, might be said of a man who, as the ages run, has hardly gone from among us.

Lincoln, one of the greatest of observers, was himself the least truly observed. God had built him in the backyard of the nation and there, wrapped in homely guise, had preserved and matured his pure humanity. He was heard, but seems rarely, if ever, to have been truly seen. The reports we have of him do not satisfy, do not justify, are inconsistent. The eastern, old-world eye could not read beyond the queer hat, bad tailoring, and boots you could not now give away—and he was so long he fairly had to stoop to look the little world in the face. Never has bad tailoring, homely, deferential manner, so completely hidden seer, jester, master of men, as did these simple accoutrements this first great gift of the West. But it is surprising that professional observers, artists and writers alike, have drawn and redrawn the untrue picture.

A great portrait is always full of compelling presence, more even than is seen in the original at all times, for a great portrait depicts great moments and carries the record of the whole man. It is, therefore, not enough to draw a mask.

Lincoln is a comfort and a reality, an example, a living inspiration to every mother and every son in America. No mask will satisfy *us*; we want to see what we care for; we want to feel the private conscience that became public conduct. We love this man, because he was all in all one of us and made all the world peers. Now we begin to see him truly. Within his coming the West has steadily rolled back the East, and of his ways the world has many. The silk hat, the tall figure, the swing, the language and manner have become American, and we all understand.

Official Washington was shocked by his address. Men, who could have given us master pictures of a master man, remained unconvinced until he had passed away. The great portrait was never drawn, and now it is too late; we must wade through mountains of material and by some strange divination find in fragments the real man, and, patiently, lovingly, yet justly, piece them all together.

It was speculation of this kind that gradually led me to a careful analysis of Lincoln the man. The *accepted* portraits of him do not justify his record. His life, his labors, his writings, made me feel some gross injustice had been done him in the blind, careless use of such phrases as *ungainly, uncouth, vulgar, rude,* which were commonly applied to him by his contemporaries. These popular descriptions do not fit the master of polished Douglas—nor the man, whose intellectual arrogance academic Sumner resented.

I believed the healthy, powerful youth and frontiersman, the lover, lawyer of spotless record, legislator, the thrice candidate for President, had been falsely drawn. I believed if properly seen and truly read, the compelling and enduring greatness of the man would be found written in his actions, in his figure, in his deportment, in his face, and that some of this compelling greatness might be gotten into the stone. To do this, I read all or nearly all he had written, his own description of himself, the few immediate records of his coming and going. I then took the life mask, learned it by heart, measured it in every possible way—for it is infallible—then returned to the habits of his mind, which his writings gave me, and I recognized that *five* or *six* of the photographs indicated the man.

Whether Lincoln sat or stood, his was the ease of movement of a figure controlled by direct and natural development, without a hint of consciousness. Chairs were low for him and so Lincoln seemed when he sat down to go farther than was quite easy or graceful. His walk was free and he moved with a long but rather slow swinging stride. His arms hung free, and he walked with an open hand. He was erect; he did not stoop at the shoulders. He bent forward, but from the waistline. His face was large in its simple masses. His head was normal in size; his forehead high, regular and ideal in shape. His brow bushed and projected like a cliff. His eyebrows were very strong. His mouth was not coarse or heavy. His right side was determined, developed, ancient. The left side was immature, plain—and physically not impressive.

You will find written in his face literally all the complexness of his nature. We see a dual nature struggling with a dual problem, delivering a single result—to the whole. He was more deeply rooted in the home principles that are keeping us together than any man who was ever asked to make his heart-beat national— too great to become president, except by some extraordinary combination of circumstances.

GUTZON BORGLUM

THEODORE ROOSEVELT

Fromentin said of Peter Paul Rubens, one of the greatest masters who ever used brush and paint to interpret human character: "He is systematic, methodical and stern in the discipline of his private life, in the ordering of his work, in the regulating of his intelligence, in a kind of strong and sane wholesomeness of his genius. He is simple, sincere, a model of loyalty to his friends, in sympathy with every one of talent, (and) untiring and resourceful in his encouragement of beginners * * *." The same might have been said with equal truth and propriety of Theodore Roosevelt.

Of all the great leaders of this country, he was the most typically American. The grief and melancholy that seized him following the death of his first wife drove him into Dakota. Here upon the range he found surcease from sorrow and sufficient time off from his duties as manager of his ranch to write about the West. This work won instant recognition and not only established his place among the literary men of his day but made him the idol of the Great West. The cowboys with whom he rode the night herd liked and admired him, and even the roughnecks soon learned to respect his cool courage and resourcefulness. One encounter with him did not give encouragement to a second.

But he was more than a frontiersman and writer. He represented all that was best in the home, in business and in government. He was energetic, intelligent and purposeful. He had an aim in life and drove hard and steadily toward his goal. His enemies seldom outmaneuvered him and he knew how to strike when a bold stroke was required to accomplish a desired end. His association with men of all types and his keen observation gave him an insight into men that enabled him to distinguish quickly and accurately the spurious from the real. Surface indications or social position had for him little meaning. He would rather associate with an uneducated but quick-witted cowpuncher than with the dull and unimaginative. This accounts for his friendship with men and women in all walks of life. Talent and ability, usefully employed, always had for him a special appeal but he was bored and annoyed by the pretentious commonplace.

He was by instinct and inclination a reformer and sought to improve all that was best in public morals, both spiritually and politically. No man struggling as mightily as he could escape making mistakes, but he was great enough to recognize them and fair enough to seek to rectify any injustice that had resulted. His enthusiasm, zeal and sureness of himself sometimes led him to pursue hopeless and occasionally ill-considered causes that he later had reason to regret, but by the large he was a most useful and inspiring personality.

Two outstanding achievements stand to his credit. One of these was the building of the Panama Canal, an accomplishment of transcendent importance to the American people. It is the link that binds the East to the West by water and has helped to make this country one of the great commercial and industrial nations of the world. The canal is also of first importance from the standpoint of national defense and has added greatly to the mobility and usefulness of our Navy, which has always been our first line of defense against any possible foreign foe.

The second was the injection of morals into our politics and the insistence upon the square deal for every American, be he small or great. It was this characteristic more than any other that endeared him to the ordinary man and made him one of the most powerful political figures and one of the greatest moral forces that has taken possession of the hearts and minds of men in any age. It was not that he was always right, but men and women clung to him because they felt that he was right most of the time and was trying to be right all of the time.

As a lone fighter he was without a peer in his day and generation, and had the impetuosity and zeal required to arouse a mighty following in any cause which he espoused and upon which he had deep convictions. Every word that he spoke and every manifestation of his personality left a profound impression upon all those who came into contact with him either personally or upon the hustings. Everywhere he was impressive, persuasive and compelling. While he may never be loved as Lincoln was loved, or rise to the stature of Washington, his example, fortitude in adversity, and fight for the betterment of his fellow men will ever be like a beacon going before to inspire men and women everywhere who are seeking to make the world a better place in which to live.

It was President Calvin Coolidge who said to Sculptor Gutzon Borglum that among the immortals to be carved upon Mount Rushmore a place must be found for Theodore Roosevelt, "because he was the first president to say to Big Business, 'thus far you shall go and no farther.'" Washington is there because he was the trusted leader that made these United States possible, and was great and strong enough to refuse a crown and lay down the scepter when his work was done. Jefferson stands at his side because of his contribution to the rights of man as set forth in the bill of rights; Abraham Lincoln because he saved the Union from division by his own martyrdom and his infinite compassion for those who suffered, and Theodore Roosevelt because he was the greatest moral force for clean government and the square deal of modern times.

WILLIAM WILLIAMSON

AS GREAT MEN SAW IT

Excerpts from speeches at dedicatory and unveiling ceremonies or comments made during personal visits to the Memorial.

President Calvin Coolidge (Consecration Ceremony, August 10, 1927)

"We have come here to dedicate a corner stone that was laid by the hand of the Almighty.... This memorial will be another national shrine to which future generations will repair to declare their continuing allegiance to independence, to self government, to freedom and to economic justice...."

President Franklin D. Roosevelt (Jefferson Unveiling)

"An inspiration for the continuance of the democratic republican form of government, not only in our own beloved country, but, we hope, throughout the world."

Lord Halifax (Visiting the Black Hills, March 29, 1946)

"The most remarkable confluence of the wonder of nature and the art of man I have ever witnessed."

Judge Albert R. Denu (Borglum Banquet, December 28, 1938)

"The historian of the future ... will record America's enduring achievements and include in his history the name of a Master Sculptor, whom the earth's inhabitants of the twentieth century knew as Gutzon Borglum."

Photograph Credits: Bell Studios, Lincoln Borglum, Charles d'Emery, Verne's Photo Shop, Publishers' Photo Service, Inc., Wyoming Department of Commerce & Industry, and Rise Studio.

MOUNT RUSHMORE NATIONAL MEMORIAL SOCIETY OF BLACK HILLS

John A. Boland, Sr.
President of Mount Rushmore National Memorial Society of Black Hills

The state of South Dakota and the community of the Black Hills have logically and with undiminished zeal accepted a considerable financial and moral responsibility in the evolution of this magnificent Shrine of Democracy.

Through the successive stages of locating, planning, sculptoring, improving and publicizing Mount Rushmore, a liaison with Sculptor Gutzon Borglum and his son, Lincoln, the President, the Congress and the Department of Interior has been maintained through the instrumentalities of three nonprofit organizations.

The Mount Harney Memorial Association was first authorized to "carve a memorial in heroic figures" under an act of Congress, approved by President Coolidge on March 4, 1925. Brought into being through a bill passed by the South Dakota Legislature, the Association entered into a formal contract with Gutzon Borglum and work was commenced in 1927.

Subsequently in 1929, when Federal funds were appropriated for matching purposes, the Mount Rushmore National Memorial Commission was created, consisting of twelve members to be named by the President.

Appointed by President Coolidge to serve on the commission were John A. Boland, Rapid City, S. D.; Charles R. Crane, New York, N. Y.; Joseph S. Cullinan, Houston, Texas; C. M. Day, Sioux Falls, S. D.; D. B. Gurney, Yankton, S. D.; Hale Holden, Chicago; Frank O. Lowden, Oregon, Ill.; Julius Rosenwald, Chicago; Fred W. Sargent, Evanston, Ill. and Mrs. Lorine Jones Spoonts, Corpus Christi, Texas.

Mr. Cullinan became the Commission's first president and Mr. Boland was named chairman of the executive committee at a session in the White House, where it met upon invitation of the President on June 6, 1929.

It was the Mount Rushmore National Memorial Commission which assumed financial responsibility for the Memorial, taking over all property and contracts from the Mount Harney Association, employing the services of a staff for the sculptor and disbursing federal and privately-solicited funds during the course of construction.

It was also the parent organization for the present Mount Rushmore National Memorial Society of Black Hills, incorporated under the laws of the District of Columbia in 1930. And while the Society's objectives were identical with those of the Commission, it had additional authority, including the sale of memberships, management of concessions and the use of available funds for advertising and publicity.

A long list of "Who's Who" in America and South Dakota have been recorded in the annals and on the membership roll of the Mount Rushmore Society. Membership certificate No. 1 is held by John Hays Hammond, world famed mining engineer, lecturer, consultant of Cecil Rhodes and active in the development of hydro-electric and irrigation projects. Number two belongs to Newton D. Baker, Secretary of War under President Wilson and a one-time member of the Permanent Court of International Justice at The Hague.

Other original members, some of whose heirs hold the certificates, are John N. Garner, vice president of the United States; Julius Rosenwald, American merchant and philanthropist; Sewell L. Avery, chain store magnate; Mary Garden, American operatic soprano; Walter Dill Scot, author and president of Northwestern University; Nicholas Murray Butler, president of Columbia University and Nobel Peace Prize winner in 1931, and Vilhjalmur Stefanson, Arctic Explorer, to mention a few.

The Society's Board of Trustees presently is composed of Paul E. Bellamy, John A. Boland, Mrs. Gutzon Borglum, Lincoln Borglum, Francis Case, Fred C. Christopherson, Miss Nina Cullinan, George E. Flavin, Mrs. William Fowden, Mrs. Peter Norbeck, Robert E. Driscoll, Sr., Eugene C. Eppley, Mrs. Frank M. Lewis and William Williamson. Walter H. Johnson is treasurer and K. F. Olsen secretary. The Commission is not active at this time.

Originally a portion of the Federal Game Sanctuary in the Harney National Forest, the 1,686-acre tract that comprises the Mount Rushmore National Memorial was established in 1929 but did not come under the National Park Service jurisdiction until 1939.

> During the interim, the South Dakota State Highway Commission constructed the present Memorial Highway from its junction with U. S. Highway 16. It also built the Iron Mountain Drive with the three tunnels that frame the Shrine of Democracy. The planning and intricate engineering skill that went into building the Iron Mountain Highway was extremely ingenious in itself.

Milton Keynes UK
Ingram Content Group UK Ltd.
UKHW042226180324
439698UK00005B/513